THE STORY OF THE MONK IN THE CELL NEXT-DOOR

The Life of Father Tadros of the
Monastery of Abba Paul, the Recluse
in the Monastery of Baramous

BISHOP MACARIUS OF MINYA

Translation by
St. Mary and St. Moses Abbey

The Story of the Monk in the Cell Next-Door: The Life of Father Tadros of the
Monastery of Abba Paul, the Recluse in the Monastery of Baramous
By Bishop Macarius of Minya

Copyright © 2025 Coptic Orthodox Diocese of the Southern U.S.A.

All rights reserved.

Designed & Published by:
St. Mary & St. Moses Abbey Press
101 S Vista Dr, Sandia, TX 78383
stmabbeypress.com

All Scripture quotations in the footnotes of this book, unless otherwise
indicated, are taken from the New King James Version® Copyright © 1982 by
Thomas Nelson, Inc. Used by permission. All rights reserved.

Contents

Introduction	5
CHAPTER ONE Monastic Ways of Life	8
CHAPTER TWO His Upbringing and Monasticism	12
CHAPTER THREE His Life in the Monastery of Baramous	30
CHAPTER FOUR His Final Days and His Repose	64
CHAPTER FIVE Examples of Recluses	72

Introduction

I spent many years relentlessly attempting to gather information about him from the fathers, especially from those who were interested in the manner of his life and his unique conduct throughout the seventeen years he spent in the monastery [of Baramous]. I was especially helped by my living in a cell adjacent to his for the last ten years of his life, where I had the opportunity to closely follow his prayers and praises and manner of life. I was interested in these, so I observed many of his actions, his reactions, and his interactions with the fathers around him. I also drew the rest of the information from his family members, whether in his town where he lived before his monasticism, or Shubra Al-Kheima, or Alwaili. Besides these, we had lengthy conversations together twice or three times under rare circumstances which did not recur, in which he declared to me many secrets and private aspects of his life, which not many had occasion to stop at [and consider].

I cannot admit his sainthood, nor do I here declare

him a contemporary righteous [man]. For this matter is left to the shrewd Church, which is inspired by the Holy Spirit, and which admits the sainthood of a person after fifty years have passed to their departure. And so, what has settled concerning him is only the truth, after most of the people who were his contemporaries have departed, and consequently all the opinions and personal impressions have [also] faded away. Also, the title of sainthood is of no benefit to him now, as much as imitating him is what benefits the living and those whom the Church asks, for he is worthy of this—that is, of being an example to imitate—because he is saintly.

Fr. Tadros of the Monastery of Abba Paul has left us a rare example of the discipline of the recluse monk, and [an example through] his love for prayer and unceasing praise, and of indescribable asceticism, and of [living as an] exile to the point of death.

As for having weaknesses, he was like all humankind who have not reached the degree of absolute perfection, an attribute ascribed only to God and no other. As for the perfection of men, it is a relative perfection, and their holiness, if compared to God's holiness, is a relative holiness also.

We ask that he pray for our sakes, that we may fulfill the days of our pilgrimage in peace, after we have accomplished that for which we are called, of holiness and righteousness. Through the prayers of

His Holiness Pope Shenouda III, who ardently loved the life of solitude and contemplation, and lived [in] it for years, before God called him to shepherd His holy Church; and also his partner in the apostolic liturgy, His Grace Abba Isizorus, who bears a special honor for this father, and he has reviewed this book. And to our God be the glory, always and forever. Amen.

Bishop Macarius of Minya

1

Monastic Ways of Life

Within the monastic framework there are many ways, and let us call them ways, rather than degrees or ranks. For monasticism itself is not a church or ecclesiastical rank; rather it is a manner of life that a person pursues. Among these ways, there are the following.

The cenobite is a monk who lives in a cell within a monastery, among the cells of the monks. Rather than having separate solitary cells, the contemporary systems in monasteries in Egypt tend now to make the cells closer to being like a complex building, on condition that these building complexes be far from where visitors and the facilities of their services are. The cenobite is committed to the daily work and the daily liturgical participation with the rest of the monks, such as Midnight Praises, the [Divine] Liturgy, and the Prayers of the Hours [Vespers]. He also eats his food—two meals each day—at the fellowship table with them, while during the remaining time, he adheres to his cell, to fulfill his spiritual canon, of prayer, prostrations, and reading spiritual books.

The solitary or hermit is the monk who began little by little to separate himself, to be alone, within the monastery itself, in coordination with the abbot of the monastery, on the condition that he has acquired the virtues of the cenobium, such as obedience, endurance, silence, faithfulness; so that these would encourage the abbot of the monastery to transfer him to the life of solitude, where he would follow a spiritual rule that is more strenuous, regarding prayers, prostrations, the type of food and its quantity, the type of reading, fasting and its degree. He also works in his cave, whether in copying books, making leather crosses, painting, or any other suitable work. He comes from time to time to partake of the Holy Mysteries in the monastery, while the monastery provides for his needs once a week.

The anchorite[1] is a solitary who, by being alone, becomes attracted toward an even greater liberty from place and possessions. The solitary, holding his staff, goes out for a walk in the desert in the evening every day, until one day he dares to spend his night in the open air while taking his walk! He finds in this delight and freedom and liberation from

---

1   We use this term to translate the Arabic word *al-sa'ih*.

some bonds. He repeats the attempt, spending more than one night wandering in the desert, until a day comes wherein he takes his staff and some bread and water and goes out of his cave, never to turn back again. Rather he spends his life walking, spending the night anywhere, getting provisions of food and water whenever there is an opportunity along the way. And from time to time he might turn and walk into a church where no one knows him, to pray and partake of the Mysteries, and he might meet others pursuing the same manner of life, and so they pray together, but in the end, he has no fixed place, no regular food, and consequently no possessions whatsoever. He is an ordinary man; he might get sick and might get hungry, but his passion for the divine things and his enjoyment in conversing with God, make food, clothing, and sleep secondary, which he does not weary his mind with. Hundreds of them, or perhaps thousands, have lived and passed away from this world without anyone being aware of them.

The recluse[2] is the monk who continues to live in a monastery, but he adheres to his cell and does not go out of it. He does not sever his ties with the community; rather he follows the discipline of the solitary while he is in his cell. This discipline is exceedingly more difficult than solitude. For the solitary naturally lives far away from events and does not meet anyone, while the recluse lives in the midst of events, but he restrains his thought

---

2   Or: shut-in.

from interacting with them. While the solitary finds an opportunity to go out into the desert, to walk and pray and meditate, we find that the recluse does not leave his cell. And so days or weeks might pass, without anyone seeing him outside his cell. Nevertheless, the recluse is committed to the same rule as the solitary, regarding prayer, fasting, prostrations, reading, and work.

There are other ascetical ways, but very sadly we do not have enough information about the conduct and rule they entail, like the worshippers[3], the ascetics, the cross-mantled, the beholders of God (Cop. *theorimos*, ⲑⲉⲱⲣⲓⲙⲟⲥ). All these may be names and indications for the ways we have mentioned, but the matter needs research and study.

I have chosen for the discipline of the recluse this contemporary example. It is rare and might not occur again in the near future.

---

3   Or: servants of God.

2

His Upbringing & Monasticism

The child Najeeb Raphael Wahbat-Allah—that is Fr. Tadros' name before monasticism—was born in Upper Egypt, specifically in the village of Majabra, which is at a distance of just over four miles[4] from the center and city of Girga which belongs to the governorate of Suhaj. This was on the 18th of June 1918.

He was raised in a simple and poor family; nevertheless, they were godly, rich through the dwelling of Christ among them. We will be assured of this in the following pages, especially that another person from the family became a monk, and that more than one person was called for the priesthood. As for the teaching he received, it was through the method customary at that time, that is the church school. This resembles the ancient

---

4   Text: seven kilometers.

Jewish synagogues, where the rabbi would teach the young boys the spiritual principles, along with memorizing the psalms of David the prophet, and [would give them] lessons in the Law and the other sciences. The church school was the common method, before the establishment of Sunday school a century ago. The person in charge of the church school was one of the educated blind men, who used to receive the children from when they were five or six years old. He would begin an arduous journey with them, through which he would teach them the principles of the Coptic language, the psalms of David the prophet, a little of the religious sciences, and the principles of the Church. As for those who showed signs of intelligence and talent, he would give them greater attention and care, taking pride and ascribing their success to his own skills.

The child Najeeb learned the psalms by heart, under the instructor Shokkri Gad-Allah, the cantor of the church there. And the cantor says about this child that he was touched by the satisfying words of God; that in them he felt a cool dew that touched the bottom of his heart, and so he clung to them; that through them he knew the path to God, and so he drank from that bottomless spring. The church became his first home, and his inclinations toward the church became the dominant direction for him, giving him an abundance of calmness, prudence, and kindness, of which his peers and neighbors sang.

The reverend hegumen, Fr. Antony Shakker, the

priest of the church in Majabra, says that Najeeb grew into a young man who was to be emulated in the village. He worked with his father in agriculture, content with what he received of education, and with his ability to read and to learn, which made him capable of studying the Holy Scriptures, praising with the Psalmody Book, praying with the Agpeya, [obtaining] consolation from reading the lives of the saints. The family owned about 2,500 square yards[5] of cultivated land, which he assumed the responsibility of continuing to cultivate, to ensure that his family continued to have something to eat. Perhaps that land was the entire inheritance of the family, which then fell to him, and perhaps it was his personal portion, as it will come up in the conversation when he left the world, heading for the wilderness.

Generally speaking, the occupation of a farmer in the rural region of Egypt aids him in acquiring a simple, strong faith, for he accompanies and follows the growth of a seed, and in this, there is a cause for praising and meditation. It is also a field for prayer and an intimate relationship with God. And this gives it, of course, the characteristic of submission to God and faith in His power and generosity altogether. These were undoubtedly among the factors forming his spiritual and liturgical personality, as we will see. It is said that he constantly bore the biggest

---

5   Text: 2,100 square meters.

burden in the responsibility of caring for that land, in contrast with his brothers and sisters. So did Najeeb Raphael grow up.

His Life Within the House and Among the Members of his Family

While Najeeb was accustomed to reciting and repeating, in the field, what he had memorized of the Holy Scriptures, as soon as he returned from his work there, he would seek refuge in his own room, which was very much like a cell, although some of the family's possessions shared it with him, a thing that made their coming in on him from time to time evident and inevitable. He would accept this reluctantly yet without grumbling. Nevertheless, little by little, these possessions began leaving his room, so that he may settle alone in it, without a partner, and consequently without disturbance. And so, the first model of a monk's cell was formed for him, and the cell, in which he lived in the first era of his monasticism, was not very different from this. Although he preserved for his room in the house the honor, the privacy, and the sanctity of the cell, the only difference was that it was among other rooms and amidst the unceasing movements throughout the day and some of the night.

In it he found his true comfort after the toil of work, and he also regained the purity of his mind after it was muddled by the cloud of the day, of what he had heard from his peers, whose cares and conversations he perceived to be at odds with his purposes and directions.

He himself related to me that he used to stay in his room the whole time. And if a guest came to visit him personally, or to visit his family in general, he would leave his place to welcome him, and spend some time with him, offering him what is proper, of the expressions of honor and welcoming of the guest. If the visit of the guest lasted long, he would excuse himself to retire, leaving the guest with the remaining members of the family, so that he may retrace his steps back to his "cell," to undertake what he had begun, whether it be prayer or reading.

Some, however, were displeased by his conduct, being treated in this manner, but soon they got used to this [behavior] from him, accepting it with contentment and understanding. He could not be with God and with them at the same time, and this was the response of Abba Arsenius the Great when the fathers entreated him to leave his solitude and live among them, and he said, "God knows that I love you, but I cannot be both with God and with men."[6] Fr. Tadros' conduct was not a lack of love for men, for we also know, according to the testimony of both the village's priest and his family members, that he often sacrificed [his] effort and money for

---

6   *The Paradise of the Holy Fathers* 2, Budge A.W., trans. (London, UK: Chatto & Windus, 1907), 14.

the sake of the poor and needy.

However, there must not be "courtesy" when the matter is concerned with the salvation of the soul. For we have received from the fathers, that at the hesitation of making a choice, we should say, "We ought to obey God rather than men."[7] And perhaps the true reason for his aversion to the idea of marriage, despite the marriage of his siblings, is that he perceived that marriage would diminish the time he used to spend with God, and that the worries of the world might choke him. Also it is marvelous that he did not set out to monasticism quickly, where it is conventional that this step be done when one is in their twenties; nevertheless, he lived as a monk in his house. And when he became a monk, we find that he lived as a solitary in the midst of the fathers of the monastery. We read in the life stories of the Ethiopian monastic saints, that some of them spent their lives in their homes and among the members of their family.

He desired, while still in the world, to visit the holy places, wishing to be blessed by these places which the Lord Christ blessed by being in them and leaving His mark on them. Therefore, he went there; and he rejoiced and was consoled by all that he saw, from the humbleness of the cradle to the light of the resurrection. And so his heart was illuminated by a new light, and his senses, his feelings, his thoughts,

---

7   Acts 5:29.

his body, and his whole being were sanctified. Then he came back, [now] called the blessed Najeeb, after a journey that added much to him. And he began joyfully relating to the people of his town all the things which he saw there, and they were touched. We also know that all the Ethiopian monks put it in their hearts to visit Egypt and then the holy places, before their death.

In his village, he was known for his love for silence, calmness, and minimal movement. The people of his village found in him a good example of the various aspects of life. He used to fast daily until sunset and then be satisfied with a simple and little amount of food, despite the arduous labor that he exerted during the day in agricultural works. Concerning his prayer, his family members testify that he used to spend a big part of the night in prayer. As for his temperament, it tended to roughness from time to time, which is attributed to human weakness, as we have aforesaid; for every one of us has weaknesses, and while the weaknesses of someone might be made manifest spontaneously in their conduct, someone else might endeavor to hide them from others. In the ascetical dispensation[8], we know that the person who is judged for a sin he committed, it is forgiven him, for this is accounted for him a public confession, while the sin of judging [another] falls upon the person who judged. God knows our nature and pities our weaknesses; He fights for us and is

---

8   Or: economy.

long-suffering with us. And it is true that through the work of grace, with struggling, a person can be saved from the old man; nevertheless, a person—any person—leaves this world while they still have a remnant of their weaknesses, but everyone who struggles is accounted victorious!

In battles, a soldier might fight unto death, so he becomes worthy of the honor befitting a faithful soldier, who loves his country. And he receives medals, and his name is recorded in the honor list, regardless of whether the whole army has gained victory or not. On the other hand, another might flee from the battle and retreat from the front line, and so he would be condemned even if his army were victorious. Likewise, a person is asked to struggle according to their ability, and so they are crowned.

"Repay No One Evil for Evil"[9]

Concerning him the people of his village relate an incident that happened to him in his life. Some evil men burned his land which was planted, so the fire destroyed half of its area. Consequently, anger was stirred in his brothers, who thought of returning the evil upon those who did so, but the blessed Najeeb refused this course and prevented his brothers from returning the evil, declaring that it has nothing to do with Christian conduct. For here God says,

---

9   Romans 12:17.

"'Vengeance is Mine, I will repay,' says the Lord."[10] And it happened that the person, who had brought about that cruel act and that plot, was stung by a venomous scorpion while he was in the field, a matter which led to his death that same week.

Not only was this so, but it was also said about Najeeb that if someone said something inappropriate in front of him, he would withdraw from that place quietly. So was it related about St. John the Short, that while he was traveling with a company of camels, which carried the work of the fathers' hands, he heard two camel drivers singing mischievous songs; so he abandoned that company. And another father was traveling with a company like this, and finding that anger stirred in the camel driver, he at once left him and went back to his cell.[11]

So Why Then did he not Become a Monk Earlier in Life?

Concerning this he himself answers, saying that he did not find a mentionable difference between completing his life the way he pursued in his environment and his room, and joining one of the monasteries. And so he began postponing that step as time went on, and when those close to him importuned him to specify his direction [in life] and

---

10 Romans 12:19.
11 See *Give Me a Word: The Alphabetical Sayings of the Desert Fathers*, Wortley J., trans. (Yonkers, NY: SVS Press, 2014), John Colobos 5.

make a decision regarding this, he answered them that he intended to go to the wilderness after the departure of his mother from this world, for he felt that he was responsible for providing for his kind mother who was a widow.

And so he continued in this marvelous manner of life. The room, in which he used to stay, is still present in his house, and it was as a cell to him. It was built with mud brick and was roofed over with palm leaves, its area being about eight by eight feet, and it is like the rest of the facilities of the home where he lived with his family. As for his cover, it was a threadbare blanket. It was possible for him to live in a manner more comfortable and luxurious, but he preferred a life of asceticism and voluntary poverty. Also from an early time, he was accustomed to sleeping facing the east, which is an ancient tradition that is more strictly observed in the monastic life.

Concerning his love for the Church, he strove to learn the Coptic language, which made him able to memorize the annual Koiahk Psalmody. Also, he used to spend long hours in the church of St. Shenouda the Archimandrite in his town, between the Offerings of Incense, the [Divine] Liturgies, and the Sunday Midnight Praises which was prayed on every Saturday evening, and he especially loved hymns for our Lady the Virgin, as we will see. Others testify of him that he would never speak in church, but rather he remained standing silently and with reverence throughout the time. And this is the habit that he followed more strictly after he became a monk. And as soon as the Divine Liturgy or the other prayers ended, he would immediately head home, where his cell awaited him, and so did he, for both waited for each other longingly.

As for the service that he did, it was caring for the poor and orphans, wherein he spent the money he had saved on this excellent work, which gladdens God's heart: "Assuredly, I say to you, inasmuch as you did it to one of the least of these My brethren, you did it to Me."[12] Nevertheless, he faced problems and many insults, especially when he asked the rich people of the village to contribute to the needs of the poor; therefore, he preferred to work in that field secretly.

As for his close friends, they were the hegumen Fr. Solomon of St. Anthony, who was present in town at that time, and the instructor Shokkri the cantor of the church, unto both of whom he was discipled, and he learned much from them.[13]

---

12 Matthew 25:40.

13 Hegumen Solomon of St. Anthony is the son of the instructor Shokkri, mentioned here. And he is also the brother of Hegumen Antony Shokkri, who is residing now in the Monastery of St. Anthony. And he is also the son of the aunt of Fr. Tadros of Abba Paul.

Leaving the World and Heading for the Wilderness

His mother passed away, and he felt that he had done for her what he owed, of the duties required by loyalty, sonship, and truth. And then he began to think about putting his desire, to move into the wilderness, into effect, there being no obstacle left. Although he could have become a monk a long while before that time, leaving his mother to the care of his other brothers, he preferred not to break her heart and reject her request of him remaining with her.

In Coptic monasteries now, the fathers and abbots of monasteries observe such aspects, encouraging those seeking monasticism to perform what the duty and commandment impose concerning honoring the parents, as much as possible, especially whenever the young man or woman were their mother's only child. They consider the brother's taking care of his own [family] a virtue, and a struggle as well, except when the mother's attachment to her son is excessive in a pathological way, and [when] there is someone else who could perform this role.

At the age of fifty, Najeeb left his village, heading for the wilderness to become a monk. He left behind in his room all that he possessed, that is, an old edition of the Holy Bible, which was published in Beirut at the end of the nineteenth century, and it is the copy that is still in his room to this day; also one of his threadbare clothes. He used to wear a simple tunic, of faded black color.

His sister-in-law says that throughout the ten years which she lived in that house, never did she hear from him a word that upset her, not even an idle word in general, to the extent that she felt that he lived as a stranger in that house. And this is the same course which he followed in the Monastery of Baramous until his death. And so he had a good impact on the house he stayed in, in particular, and the town he lived in, in general.

A Vision in His Room

After he left the world and headed for the wilderness, his niece, Nivene, went into the room where he was staying. She was surprised by a man wearing white clothes, facing the east, praying, and the fragrance of incense filled the place. She was at that time not older than five. So she went to her mother, relating to her what she had seen, and all those who heard this marveled.

Najeeb left his village, heading for the headquarters of the monasteries of Abba Anthony and Abba Paul in the village of Boush, Beni Swef governorate, to seek monasticism in the Monastery of Abba Paul. In this, he was following the advice of his cousin the hegumen, Fr. Solomon of the Monastery of Abba Anthony, who advised him not to become a monk in the Monastery of Abba Anthony, that the familiarity between them—because of kinship and friendship—might not hinder them from the goal which both of them went out in pursuit of. Until this day there are some fathers of monasticism who do not approve of two brothers becoming monks in one monastery, or any two who are related to each other—and this is for the same reason. Nevertheless, spiritual friendships between those who are not related have formed within the monastic frame, in a stronger and firmer manner than that if they were brothers or kin. Also, this is a praise-worthy matter in monasticism. On this, we have many duos in monastic history, who are to be imitated, such as St. Maximus and St. Dometius, St. Apollo and St. Apip, St. Cosman and St. Damian, St. Pishoy and St. Paul of Tammoh, and many others.

Despite that Najeeb joined the monastery at an advanced age, he proved himself courageous in his struggle. And the suitable age for monasticism, with respect to young men, is between twenty-five and thirty; for readiness for work, toil, and struggling are greater [at such ages]. Also by this, the monk would have given as a gift to Christ the most precious of what he owns: that is, his youth. Adding to this is that the person who tarries for too long to join the monastery gives an opportunity for more worldly experiences, incidents, and interactions, which take place during his presence in the world; these would disturb him in his monastic life and would draw him backward from time to time.

This father, however, broke this rule, confirming through practical proof that if the love of Christ reigned in the heart, it would overcome all difficulties. Consequently, the heaviest commandments become easy and light, and this is with the assurance of the presence of a will linked to love. Fr. Tadros was faithful in his spiritual rule until the last day, before an illness took him by surprise three days before he reposed so quietly that it afterward caught the attention of all.

On the Outskirts of Life in the Monastery

Concerning the first period of his monastic life, he himself related that they had charged him with staying in the field belonging to the monastery in Boush village, to oversee the farmers and to care for the crops. And this custom is still followed until today with respect to the monasteries that have properties of agricultural lands, where one of the fathers is charged with this, and some novices, who desire [to pursue] the ascetical life, help him by way of testing. Najeeb stayed in the field or nearby, for a period of a year and a half. And he related, with much bitterness and grief, what he encountered from the farmers there, of ill-treatment while he was there. He even lacked bread and water at times. But this perhaps occurred because of his strictness and faithfulness, which incited their hatred and slander.

On account of his previous experience in the field of agriculture, for a period exceeding forty years, he was aware of everything that was going on, and consequently, deceiving him was not easy. And he did not approve of any negligence or stealing. This was for him a cause of constant conflict with the farmers and workers there.

Finally, they permitted him into the monastery, to leave the field and join the community of the monastery,[14] whose abbot at that time was the late Abba Arsenius, the bishop of the monastery, and this was in 1969. A few months after his arrival he was tonsured as a monk by the late Hegumen Basilius, the steward of the monastery, who had this authority at that time, and he named him "Tadros," meaning "the gift of God."

There he lived in the monastery for four years before leaving it for the Monastery of Baramous. During that period there, he was a contemporary of Fr. Pachom of Baramous, who lived for nine years there and who worked at that time as an assistant of the steward of the monastery, Hegumen Basilius of

---

14   Here is an example of how a young man was tested before allowing him into the monastery: It happened in the residence of the Monastery of Abba Samuel that a young man came to the late Abba Mina, the abbot of the monastery at that time, asking to be accepted for monasticism. But he was asked to remove the corn kernels from a huge quantity of corn cobs, which filled a whole room. This was done to test his patience and obedience. This was what the brother precisely did, calmly and meekly, without being wearied for three whole days without interruption; and then he rejoiced in him and tonsured him as a monk.

the Monastery of Abba Paul, and the total number of monks in the monastery did not exceed ten monks, and consequently, he supervised him in his work. As for the work, it was caring for a humble chicken farm, which was basically a rear room that accommodated no more than twenty chickens; and also making Corban[15]. The making Corban used to be assigned every month to one of the fathers or brothers, as is the case for us in the Monastery of Baramous, in that the brothers, who are seeking monasticism, monthly take turns to make Corban, but if their number were small, then some of the new monks are added to the list.

It is known that Fr. Tadros was experienced and skilled in this work, and he worked for a long time in making Corban in the Monastery of Baramous. And until his repose, he would express his precious observations and would offer advice to the person making it.

And while he was in the Monastery of Abba Paul, the number of monks went down, from ten to four monks only, for six of them left the monastery, going to the Patriarch, while the following continued in the monastery: Hegumen Abd El Said, Hegumen Fannous, Hegumen Abdel Massih, Fr. Tadros himself, and Fr. Pachom of the Monastery of Baramous.

One day he protested to those in charge in the

---

15 The bread used in the Divine Liturgy.

monastery, because [the quality of] the flour which he used to make Corban was bad, and he demanded that good flour be brought instead. But they rejected that, perhaps because of the lack of means, or perhaps because of the rarity that such things arrive at the monastery. Nevertheless, these disagreements of his were childlike and did not reflect [the existence of] any evil in him, nor hatred or pride, as evidenced by him not harboring hatred or grudges against anyone, for minutes later he would be seen as though nothing at all had happened.

Whatever the reasons were, his soul was embittered, and he could no longer bear it, and he renounced the idea of remaining in his monastery. And this he asked of the steward of the monastery, who in turn informed the late Abba Agathon, Metropolitan of Ismailia, whom His Holiness the Pope had appointed as overseer of the monastery. And there, at the patriarchate building, a discussion went on between him and the metropolitan, at the end of which he also insisted on leaving the Monastery of Abba Paul. And when they presented the matter to H.H. the Pope, he consented to his request and sent him to the Monastery of Baramous, and this was in 1973.

3

His Life in the Monastery of Baramous

His Arrival at the Monastery of Baramous

Fr. Tadros arrived at the Monastery of Baramous in the second half of 1973. The monastery consisted of twenty-five monks at that time, including some elders such as Hegumen Makkar (†1993), Hegumen Abdel Massih (†1978), Hegumen Tanago (†1981), Fr. Moussa (†1988), and Fr. Ibrahim (†1993). The economus of the monastery at that time was Hegumen Manasseh of Baramous (†1991).

At the beginning of his monastic life, he used to copy the Holy Scriptures and the Agpeya, and sell them, but he afterward focused on studying the Holy Scriptures themselves.

The first work he was entrusted with in the

monastery was making Corban. He was honest in his work, as we have seen, and he continued in this work for several years. When the number of the fathers increased in the years following his arrival, especially after 1975 when His Holiness Pope Shenouda III sent a group of monks to restore the monastery and revive it,[16] others were entrusted with making the Corban, out of compassion for him because of his advanced age. At this, he contented himself with passing, now and then, by "Bethlehem," the place where the Corban was made; soon, however, his cell drew him in. That cell, which he was given, was located directly beside the fort of the monastery, on the north-western side. And it was in this cell, which he did not leave until his death, that he lived as a recluse. And Fr. Isaac of Baramous currently lives in it.

The Elderly Warrior

This father, living as a recluse, is considered one of the rare examples of this manner of life. We observed him closely, we who lived in the cells near his. He used to rebuke us through his conduct. And I remember that we would spend long nights, being unable to sleep because of the many [spiritual]

---

[16] These were H.G. Abba Arsenius, Bishop of Minya, H.G. Abba Antonious Markos, Bishop of African Affairs, H.G. Abba Yacobus, Bishop of Zagazig, H.G. Abba Benyamin, Bishop of Menofia, and Hegumen Palladius of the Monastery of the Syrians.

struggles which he carried out in a way that was obvious to us, especially on the extremely hot summer nights when he would have to keep the door of his cell ajar. And because of the rebuke, we could not sleep. Nevertheless, what caused us more pain was our inability to transform the rebuke of our consciences to emulation of him, of his manner of life. He started his ritual when most of the fathers in the monastery were asleep, while he would sleep for a short while when we were busy with our various works during the day.

He was rarely seen outside his cell. He was known for his traditional, familiar look, by all those who were his contemporaries: he was tall in stature, thin in body, his head permanently lowered down. He wore clothes that were worn to shreds and were patched with colors other than black, ranging between green and blue, and he walked with such slowness that was unsurpassed. And if one of the fathers greeted him, he would greet him back without turning to him; and when we entreated him, saying, "Your prayers, our father Tadros," his head still lowered down, he would answer, "The prayers of the fathers and the saints," and at other times he would answer, "But the one who accepts," that is to say, "Would God accept it from me?" He means, of course, that he prayed a lot, but if only God would accept his entreaties.

Generally, he is considered a unique personality in his character, the like of whom is unlikely to be found. He lived in silence and stillness, throwing around himself a fence of utter secrecy, and he absolutely did not permit anyone whatsoever to break through this barrier, even those who thought that they were close to him or that they had boldness with him. Therefore, it was not easy at all for a person to discover his rule of life. Also, he did not have a father of confession in the monastery; rather, his father of confession was His Eminence Metropolitan Mina, Metropolitan of Girga—may God prolong his life. And of course this he did—that is confession—once a year or so, during his visit to his family.[17] It might be suitable to mention now the following incident.

Fr. Roweis of Baramous recounted, saying: I noticed Fr. Tadros' absence from the refectory for two successive days. Therefore, without being asked by anyone to do so, I went on my own accord and gently knocked on his door. When he asked about who it was that was knocking, I took the initiative and asked him why he had not come to the refectory and consequently whether he needed food. He answered from inside, asking for a piece of bread, one boiled egg, and a cup of tea. I asked his permission to bring two eggs, and he consented.

---

17 It was not easy for a monk's family to come for a visit in the previous generation, because of the ruggedness of the way and the long distance, especially with respect to those who were from Upper Egypt. Consequently, most monks used to go to their families for few days once a year, usually during the Holy Fifty period.

And so I went away, and a little while later I came back, carrying the things he needed. I knocked on his door, and he opened the door and came out quietly, then he shut the door behind him before sitting on the ground, and I sat across from him. He broke the bread in a plate and poured the tea on it, and then he began to eat from the plate and from the eggs together. And before I had the chance to ask him about the reason for his absence, he himself started by saying, "I had wanted to partake [of the Mysteries], and I was prepared and had confessed, but the filthy one [meaning the devil] hindered me from doing so." I kept silent, and so did he. And as soon as he finished his food, I excused myself and walked away.

When I met my father of confession, he asked me why I was sitting with Fr. Tadros. I told him the whole story, and then he asked me not to do this again, in fear that I break his spiritual rule, whether that of seclusion or asceticism.

Several things may be noted here. First, he did not have a spiritual father in the monastery, so where and how did he confess that day? And it may seem surprising that the devil wars against a monk to the last minute of his life. For Fr. Tadros often suffered from sudden pain. Also, he had been fasting for two successive days, and they could have been extended if it had not been for the father who came to check on him. And when food was offered to him, he consented in simplicity.

And we knew nothing about him, except what was made possible to us through fleeting incidents outside his cell. He, however, had no dealings with the fathers, except two people whom he knew by name: one of them was the father responsible for the storage of the monastery, who was Fr. Bishoy (H.G. Bishop Isizorus now), and he used to call him, "Bishai," and after him Fr. Agathon; as for the second person, it was Fr. Seraphim of Baramous (H.G. Abba Seraphim, Bishop of Ismailia). In addition to these, there were two other persons, whom he only knew by their titles, without there being a need for him to memorize their names: and these were the abbot of the monastery and the economus[18] of the monastery.

H.G. Bishop Isizorus said that when he received the grace of the priesthood, Fr. Tadros visited him to congratulate him, and he had a cup of tea with him. It was the only time he entered his cell. And I remember that when he heard that H.G. Abba Agathon was no longer the abbot of the Monastery of Abba Paul, he asked in simplicity, saying, "Who, I wonder, is now responsible for the storage of the monastery?" and it is clear that he had forgotten all about Abba Agathon—and also the Monastery of Abba Paul, and no sooner did he hear the name "Agathon" than his thought went to the storage of the monastery [who was named Fr. Agathon].

We, however, know his rule of prayer and praise,

---

18 I.e., trustee.

being fulfilled audibly, for he felt that no one was observing him. And this was in the night only; as for the day, we did not hear him, of course. Neither do we know anything about his own personal prayers and his arrow prayers.

I remember that one day he needed the father who was responsible for the clinic, and although he knew his name, he had forgotten it. And he referred to me, and there was another [father] with me, saying, "I want father..." and he was silent, and so we began listing to him the names of the fathers in the monastery until he stopped [us] at Fr. Seraphim. And on another occasion, he needed something from the economus of the monastery, and he asked us, "Where is he and what is his name?" and when we said that it was Fr. Sedrak, he asked us to help him meet him. When he met him, he reproached him for having not yet fulfilled a matter for him which he had sent him.

He did not care about anyone and had familiarity with nobody. One person, however, was able to break through his silence several times, who dared to joke with him, making him talk and laugh; nevertheless, this also was done with brevity, and soon he would regain his calmness and gravity, his countenance being shrouded with seriousness once again.[19]

---

19 The following amusing story is recounted concerning Abba Pambo. When the demons perceived his seriousness and strictness, they wanted to trick him, to make him laugh, for he was not in the habit of doing that. So they brought a bird before him, and bound its foot with

His Daily Program

Fr. Tadros' day started at nine p.m., washing his face and preparing the battery-powered flashlight, which he used to call "the searcher." Then he would prepare his sitting area in his cell, which consisted of a sackcloth sack, placing this on the ground next to the door from inside, on which he put his Psalmody book. And the light in the entire monastery was no sooner turned off at ten p.m. (at that time) than he started praying the Midnight Hour Prayer, reciting it leisurely, word by word, with a tune, slowly. And he had no problem, now and then, to repeat a phrase which he had interacted with. And I remember that he frequently stopped at the phrase "save us and have mercy on us," and he did not mind repeating it about twenty times, with delight and joy, and with a tune, and after each time he would comment something from himself like, "O my beloved Jesus," or, "Amen, Jesus," or others, this indicating that his work was not done for the sake of fulfilling a rigid canon, as a necessary duty; rather, he used to delight in his prayer, interacting with its words. For it was not important for him *when* he would finish his

---

a string, and then they began to move it in an eye-catching manner—and behold, the saint laughed! And at this the demons rejoiced, crying out, for they had finally succeeded in making him laugh. But he looked at them, mockingly, saying, "Yes, I laughed, but at your worthlessness and great emptiness. Otherwise, you would not have gathered in such a number to make me laugh.... Do you understand why I laughed?" And so they departed from him disappointed once again.

prayer, but *how* he would enjoy it and be comforted by it. Prayer for him was an easy, beloved work.

Once he finished praying the psalms—which took him an hour and a half to two hours—then he began the Midnight Praises, reciting it in the same way it is recited in church, yet leisurely, pausing between one stanza and another. And when he reached the Commemoration of the Saints, he would add some names which were not usually chanted in the Psalmody [book]. It was also noted that he still mentioned H.E. Abba Mina, the metropolitan of his diocese, although he had left it a long time prior. And from this, then, we understood that he was not bound by time.

Some days he used to go out to the bathroom, which was about twenty-two yards from his cell,[20] and that was done between the segments of his spiritual vigil. And so he would finish the Midnight Praises at three or three-thirty in the morning, at which time the monastery's bell would ring, announcing the beginning of the Midnight Prayer.

And then he would start, still in his cell also, praying the psalms of the Morning Hour, in the same way he prayed the Midnight Hour, with delight and very attentively, taking nearly an hour to finish it. After this comes the Morning Doxology, which went on for more than half an hour. At this point, the time would be five or five-thirty in the morning, and so

---

20 Text: twenty meters.

the voice would go silent, and we would think that he had finished his vigil and program; yet, lo and behold, he would begin reciting the Book of Job in the *Adrebe* or mournful tune,[21] reading all of it in a way similar to how the Lamentations of Jeremiah is recited at the end of Great Friday, and this would take him about two hours! We are regretful that we did not record his recital, for, a short while after his repose, we learned that there is a way for reciting the Book of Job. This was known to the old learned [people] in Upper Egypt, and there is an indication to this tune in the Liturgy of St. Cyril, where it is stated that the segment "Not that we are worthy, O Master, to intercede," is said in the tune of Job, that is the tune of mourning.

At this, the time would have reached seven in the morning; that is, he had spent about nine hours in prayer, praises, and chanted reading, without interruption. With the exception of the final few years, when he had to sit on the ground because of the impairment of his health, all this was fulfilled while standing. As for the psalms, he knew them by heart, but he had to seek the help of the book and the "searcher" in some parts of the Psalmody and when reading the Book of Job the righteous.

---

21 Some see that the word "Adrebe" is attributed to the town of Athribis, where some of the mournful hymns were composed. Others believe that it belongs to the town of Adrebian in Upper Egypt. It is more likely, however, that it is derived from the Coptic word *eterheibi*, meaning "mourning."

After this, he would head for the church, extremely slowly, to attend what remained of the Divine Liturgy if he were not intending to partake of the Mysteries. However, he would go earlier whenever he desired to partake of the Mysteries, making the exception of not reading the Book of Job in its entirety. And in church, he was accustomed to standing in front of the iconostasis until the end of the Liturgy, and he was never seen sitting throughout this [time]. And as soon as he took the blessed bread (eulogia), he would return to his cell, holding it in his hand, placing it against his chest!

As for the rest of his day, he spent it on his personal affairs, such as washing what needed to be washed, cleaning the cell, eating food, and taking some sleep that, I suppose, did not exceed four or five hours. Sometimes I used to hear him praying the Third, Sixth, and Ninth Hours at midday. And while his voice was very clear during the night, it was faint or inaudible during the day. And perhaps because of our busyness too during the day, we did not follow well this part of his discipline.

His Faithfulness to his Rule of Prayer and Praising

One day in 1985, he was obliged to be at the headquarters of the monastery in Azbakeya. The monastery had one room in the building of the metropolitans, divided into four sections by fabric curtains. And he was obliged to sleep over there. For him the problem was not *where* to sleep over; rather, the true problem was *how* to fulfill his spiritual rule in that tight place. And he could find no way but the balcony of that room, which overlooked the courtyard of the church of St. Mark. And so he went onto it and completely forgot where he was, and he began to pray his psalms audibly, almost in a loud way. The fathers, who were there on that day, tried to sleep but failed. And one of them called to him, to alert him that there were some who could hear him praying, yet he paid attention to none of this. Likewise, the workers in the church down below were surprised by a monastic elder standing and praying for long hours on the balcony on the second floor. And they heard him clearly, because of the stillness of the night and the lack of movement in the place. He did not enter the room except after he had finished his rule of prayer, which was not finished before the fathers had woken up again.

His Relationship with the Holy Scriptures

Fr. Tadros was in the habit of reading the Holy Scriptures by chanting, and he generally leaned toward the mourning tune. His voice was plaintive, melodious, moving. His way [of chanting] was more like that of ballads and epics. In this, he was undoubtedly influenced by the environment in which he grew up, where praises and spiritual songs abound, those which have mystical folklore- and epic-like influence, the way he recited the Book of Job, as we have seen.

During the day, he leaned toward meditation on the Holy Scriptures—or more precisely he leaned toward "rumination." He would read a passage and then comment on it, as someone explaining to his listeners. And there is a rare recording of him, wherein he explained the matter of the killing of the firstborn of the Hebrews according to Pharaoh's command, and how the two midwives refrained from this. And he went on for two full hours, meditating on this. This rare pearl was recorded by Fr. Suriel of Baramous. When listening to it, it may be noted how he combined lightheartedness in explanation and biblical awareness.

We also once heard him explaining to himself in his cell the story of Joseph the righteous, meditating on how he had stored the grain for seven years without it becoming spoiled by worms, and so on. It was evident that he enjoyed this exceedingly, the time flying by without him noticing that. And so, each of his sittings with the Holy Scriptures lasted for hours.

Fr. Macarius of Baramous says that he once felt that Fr. Tadros, in one of his sittings with the Holy Scriptures, was as though sitting with others who were listening to him, and was as though in a Bible study meeting, for he would repeat from time to time, "Did you understand what I am saying?" or, "Is this clear?" and he was explaining fervently and emotionally.

H.G. Abba Seraphim related concerning him, saying: For a time I was responsible for the bakery, and, while I was waiting for the yeast to leaven the dough or something of this sort, I heard Fr. Tadros—for the bakery was located about thirty-three yards across from his cell. He seemed as though he was speaking with someone else. So I walked quietly to sit on a chair that was nearby. I found him washing some articles of his simple clothes, and during this, he was "ruminating" on a verse from the Holy Scriptures: "Do men gather grapes from thornbushes or figs from thistles?"[22] And this went on for two full hours or so. He would say it, then repeat it, marveling, explaining to himself that it was impossible for thornbushes to give grapes, and thistles figs. And perhaps He meant that whoever strives is crowned, and whoever does not strive does not inherit a portion in the glory—and that from its fruits we know the tree; and whatever a person sows, that he will reap; and that it is the eternal portion which a person gathers as a result of his labor and faithfulness. And this is rumination on the word of God.

---

22 Matthew 7:16.

His Food

He was not vegetarian, but rather, he ate whatever he was offered, giving thanks. If there was meat on the refectory table,[23] he would ask for only a small piece with the soup, adding some bread to it. But most frequently he would be content with pouring a cup of tea into a plate containing some bread and sugar. And it was noted that, despite the simplicity of his food, he cared very much about the cleanliness of the utensils he used and also the chair he sat on. And there seems to be no relationship between poverty and luxury[24] on the one hand and orderliness and cleanliness on the other. This is the case when he went to the refectory table of the fathers, but some other times he went to the kitchen of the monastery, because the appointed times of the refectory table did not usually suit him (ten in the morning and five in the evening). And in the kitchen, he would sit in a corner quietly and would humbly eat a little of the food he found there—beans or lentils. He would eat and would then drink a cup of tea, before returning to his cell.

When fruits or things like these were brought to the monastery, the fathers used to put his share in a small wooden box that was next to his cell, for him, in his turn, to take whenever he wished, without disturbing him. He, however, used to

---

23 Literally: on the table.
24 Or: richness.

leave them until they went bad and rotted, to be consequently thrown into the trash. One of the fathers—Fr. Pachom—learned of this, so he began taking what was in the box and distributed them to some of the workers in the monastery. And when Fr. Tadros saw him once, he said to him, "I don't mind it if you take what you find in the box of foods, but only leave the other things like clothes." And so he usually did not eat what was placed in it. And he had suffered from diabetes, but he did not care much about this; neither did he care about the type of food, for carbohydrates and sugars must be excluded. But he just ate whatever he found. And the cause of his repose was the complications of this disease, as we will see.

One morning, Fr. Elijah of Baramous, accompanied by another monk, met him in front of the kitchen of the monastery, where he was sitting to eat his food on the low fence there. Fr. Elijah asked him, "Why don't you eat meat now, father?" And he looked to him and stared at him for a long time, before giving him an answer, saying, "With red ink, sorrow is written on monasticism!" He meant that monasticism is the way of suffering, sorrow, and ascetical labor, which is an established and certain thing, and a person should not look for comfort or seek pleasure.

Then he asked him again, "I sin a lot; what do I do?" He answered, "It is fitting that you do not sin. If you do sin, let that be from the outside, not from the heart," like David the prophet who sinned and repented quickly. He means, of course, that there should not be a place for sin in the heart. Fr. Tadros himself lived according to this thought, for if he sinned or wronged someone, that was from the outside only, in that he would forget the whole matter a few minutes later, without harboring hatred against anyone in his heart.

Fr. Elijah went back to importune him, asking him about his refusal to eat meat, but this time he preferred silence, entirely ending the conversation.

And one day in early summer, I remember that I offered to fill the water clay pot that had been next to the door of his cell from outside since the previous season. He looked at me, then said, "Leave it. It is full." The clay pot was there, covered in dust, from the previous summer. Perhaps he imagined that he had just filled it—or a few hours earlier—for the time had passed quickly and he did not feel it; perhaps he thought that the water he had put in it last time was still there, but it may have even become cold water!

His Clothes

Neither I, nor others, have seen him wearing new clothes, or [even] clothes in good condition, perhaps except those clothes he wore when he went to church, which were not without some patches either. He was often seen sitting in front of the door of his cell, patching his clothes. His patched clothes were also seen hung on a [laundry] rope fixed in front of his cell. And he would sit near the door of his cell to wash his clothes in a medium-sized tub, but he did not [really] know how to wash them well, for his clothes remained as they were after the washing, to be hung [on the rope to dry]. And whoever saw them thought that they were tattered rags that were set aside for cleaning purposes. He was also often seen "attempting" to wash some sackcloth bags, yet I do not know if he used these to put some belongings in them, or to sit on them, or to wear them in his cell. In any case, he used to sit across from the hung laundry until they were dry, this scene reminding us of the scene of our father Abraham before his sacrifice, driving away the birds of prey from it!

As for the new articles of clothing he received—outerwear, underclothing, a scarf, cowls, socks—he used to keep them, without using any of them. And some of the elders of the monastery used to resent [seeing] his tattered clothes when he walked wearing them among other people, and they would rebuke him because of them, but he would walk in his way as though he heard nothing or as though the words were directed to another, and a little while later he would resume his prayers and praises as though nothing had happened, and without losing his peace.

His Love for the Cell

Since the time he had dwelled in the cell, he had not left it. It is located at the end of the row of the western cells, on the west side of the monastery, on the inner side of the wall. It is perpendicular to the row itself, while its north-western corner is attached to the ancient fort, as we have said. It consists, like all the cells, of two rooms, one inside the other, and the area of the room is about twelve square yards. It is built with cement bricks and roofed with reinforced concrete but without a mentionable foundation in the ground. And it is of "continental" conditions: scorchingly hot in the summer, and bitterly cold and damp in the winter. It has suffered from many cracks, and humidity and water have seeped in from the roof, which is not tightly sealed.

As for its contents, it had a low wooden bed in the inner room,[25] upon which a shabby mattress was placed, and had a rickety wooden chair. As for the outer room, it contained a water earthenware placed on a low metal chair, in addition to a washing tub, worn-out covers, and old beddings. On the floor, above a large sack, he had placed his copy of the Holy Scriptures on top of the Annual Holy Psalmody book and the Koiahk one. And he did not own a copy of the Agpeya.

He did not leave his cell throughout a single day, except for three cases: the first was to go to the

---

25   Inner room is called *mahbasa* in Arabic.

bathroom, and as he was going there he would carry a bucket for water with him, to bring it back filled, and when we used to ask him to carry it for him—considering his old age—he would strongly refuse; the second time was to go to church, sometimes for the Divine Liturgy or the psalms prayer in the evening; the third time was to take some food from the kitchen or the refectory back to his cell, or he may eat his food there, noting that he did not daily go out to get food.

And he had consented that Fr. Agapios—for he liked his simplicity and spontaneity—may clean his cell once a year. We remember that a small mouse snuck into his cell and enjoyed living in it, running happily here and there for a few years. And despite the disturbances it caused him, he did not dare to drive it away, but he would rebuke it in simplicity as though it were an annoying tenant. Although there is no objection to killing such insects and rodents, especially if they are harmful, when one of the fathers suggested this to him, however, he kindly rebuked him, saying, "How do I exercise dominion over him and take his life away, while my life and his are in the hand of God."[26]

Despite the simplicity of that cell, it was very neat and clean. Fr. Seraphim (H.G. Bishop

---

26 It is said concerning Fr. Abdel Massih the Ethiopian that he was peaceable even with scorpions and serpents. And when some of his visitors asked him regarding this, he answered that God had given us authority that we may escape their harm, not that we kill them.

Seraphim) related that one day Fr. Tadros needed a jar of ointment, to apply it to his left arm, which often hurt by the humidity. He had given him one a few days earlier. Therefore, he asked him if it had run out. (He asked him in the hope of making him say what could be beneficial, that is, a word of benefit). So he answered, "I put it here, but the accursed took it," and he means the devil, of course. And there was no justification for its disappearance from a neat cell, except in this way.

After his repose, he also appeared in this cell in the following way. Fr. Isaac, who lived in his place in the cell, said: One night I felt someone nudging me,[27] to wake me up. This was repeated again and again, and I was alarmed throughout the night and could not sleep. I felt his presence throughout the night, sitting next to me on the bed for a while, then walking in the cell, after that standing before an icon of the Virgin in the inner room, then leaving the cell to return to it again. With all these, there was a dim light in the cell, and I felt peace and tranquility, and I was not afraid at all. In the morning, I asked one of the fathers about what this could have been, so he was surprised that that day was the annual commemoration of Fr. Tadros' repose!

---

27 Literally: patting on.

His Death to the World

Fr. Tadros lived in the Monastery of Baramous for seventeen years, and at the time of his repose, the number of monks in the monastery had reached seventy monks. And he knew none but two or three, and what is even more [surprising] than this is that he did not know well the facilities of the monastery. One day he stood before the gate of the monastery and looked with simplicity at the church of Abba Moses the Black adjoining the monastery. Then he asked, with amazement and surprise, "When did you build that church?" The fathers, who were standing there, answered him, marveling, "It was built ten years ago!" He in turn marveled and remained silent.

With time, the recluse feels that his cell is larger than the whole outside world, and he is even constrained by the vacancy and vastness outside the cell, and he feels ill at ease as long as he is outside it, but soon, without tarrying, he returns to it, where his true rest is. And he substitutes the necessity of walking with the prostrations he makes daily every morning. And because of the stillness which he acquires, his movement gradually lessens even within the narrow cell itself. Therefore, our amazement will vanish when we read about the stylites and the recluses who spent long years without going out to meet anyone. For, look, here is a monk who dwelled in his cell for many years without seeing its ceiling;[28]

---

28   See *Give Me a Word: The Alphabetical Sayings of the Desert Fathers*,

that is, he did not occupy himself with this matter. Also, Amma Sarah lived beside the river for sixty years without going out to look at it;[29] that is, she did not go out, not even once, with the intention of passing time or sitting on its beach. Every person, who has become occupied with divine matters, who has gradually become loosed from the cares of this world, will comprehend how this is a firm truth, and not an exaggeration or excessive self-restraint.

Fr. Matthew of Baramous said that Fr. Tadros, two or three weeks before his repose, asked him to take him by car and show him all the facilities, establishments, and farms of the monastery. He consented to his request, surprised at this behavior. And he took him through all the farms, and he would inquire about the type of crops that were grown, then about the functions of the buildings, and then the roads and cells, and so on. Perhaps this happened when he sensed that the time of his repose drew near, and so he desired to bid farewell to everything in the monastery, for it was extremely rare for him to be seen outside the gate of the monastery.

The marvelous thing is that when he used to visit his village in Suhag, he would not interact with anything or anyone until he returned to the monastery once again after a while. In this, he

---

Wortley J., trans. (Yonkers, NY: SVS Press, 2014), Helladius 1.
29   Ibid., Sarah 3.

resembled Abba Isidore, the priest of Scetis, who was [once] obliged to go to Alexandria to meet Pope Theophilus, the twenty-third Pope, for some matter. When he returned to the desert, the fathers asked him about the conditions of the city, so he said to them that he had seen no one except our father, the Patriarch only. Then they asked him if he meant that the city of Alexandria was uninhabited. He said, "No, but I restrained my thought, and so I did not care about anything else."[30]

H.G. Bishop Isizorus relates concerning Fr. Tadros that after the events of September 1981, when some bishops, priests, and some members of the congregation were seized [and imprisoned], and there was a severe tribulation on the Church, he was seen to be as calm as he usually was. And he did not ask about anything, and did not follow [the progress of] the matter, nor did anyone speak to him concerning it. Therefore, he and the economus of the monastery, who was Hegumen Antonius of Baramous at that time, wanted to know how he interacted with that incident. And as he was walking, carrying something or returning to his cell, the two stopped him and asked him, with gentle disapproval, "Haven't you heard what happened?" Then they quickly related to him the incident. And so he looked at them in silence for a few moments, then he walked away, saying, "What is new in this? This is the Church throughout her history."

---

30 Ibid., Isidore of Scete 8.

And here he (Bishop Isizorus) looked to Hegumen Antonius, asking, "I wonder, did he mean to say something?" And he answered, "Yes, perhaps he is delicately reproaching us, that we may go to our cells and finish our spiritual canon."

Also if he heard the bell of the monastery ringing, he would sometimes come out to ask with a calmness that was full of seriousness whether the bell was about a church prayer or another matter, and other matters were none of his concern; otherwise, had he asked, "Why is the bell ringing?" then he would have received a detailed answer. And in 1981, the bell of the monastery continued to ring with mournful tunes for several hours—from three to eleven in the morning—for Fr. Antonius of Baramous had passed away. He finally came out of his cell, with extreme calm, and walked swiftly toward the ancient church without speaking to anyone on the way. When he walked to the front of the church, to worship before the sanctuary, he glanced and saw a box placed on a table, in which one of the fathers was lying. After he worshipped before the sanctuary and prayed, and after he worshipped before the relics also, then he asked someone who was standing there, "Who is that who is lying in the box?" And they answered him, "It is Hegumen Antonius." And he used to know him, and then he asked, simply and hurriedly, "Was he sick?" They gave him a negative answer, without telling him that he had died in a car accident. He shook his head and walked to the back of the church, where he began praying his psalms audibly, as though nothing had happened.

And when Fr. Tanago passed away, who was the oldest elder of the monastery and one of its pillars at that time, the economus of the monastery asked one of the fathers to pass by the cells [in the monastery], to inform the monks of this. When that father came to Fr. Tadros' cell, he continued to knock [on his door] for a long time, without an answer. And so he knocked harder, in case he was perhaps asleep. After about ten minutes, he opened the door and asked him disapprovingly about the dangerous matter for which he troubled him in this manner with his annoying knocking. The monk answered instantly, thinking that in his answer there was a powerful response to that disapproval and there was also a rebuke for delaying to answer [the door], and so he said that Fr. Tanago had passed away! He expected that Fr. Tadros would gasp at the news or would be shocked upon hearing that. But he answered him indifferently, as he was closing the door, "Does this matter deserve that you disturb me in this way? We are all going to die." Then he closed the door and returned to his serenity.

Some might think that, in this, there is a sort of unfriendliness and lack of sentimental participation, of which God has commanded us: "Rejoice with those who rejoice, and weep with those who weep."[31]

---

31 Romans 12:15.

He, however, participated and attended all occasions of this sort, but he rather interacted in a different way, seeing that the monk lives in anticipation of that day and that we should not be like the people of the world in such circumstances. Mar Isaac says, "A merchant fixes his eye upon dry land, and a monk upon the hour of his death."[32]

One time he asked me to call for him the father responsible for the clinic, and Fr. Seraphim came at once. He knocked on the door, and Fr. Tadros came out a few minutes later, as his custom was. When he saw that it was the doctor, he pointed to his shoulder, for it was hurting him. The father knew that it was the humidity [that caused it] and suggested that he take some pills which he would bring for him, but he asked for an adhesive dressing. Fr. Seraphim hesitated a little, before resorting to obedience and hastening to bring it for him. When he suggested to him that they go into the cell, so that he can put the adhesive dressing on for him, he protested that the cell was hot! The area in front of his cell was crowded with visitors, considering that there were bathrooms in that place, which they used. Fr. Tadros attempted earnestly to uncover his shoulder, but he could not, and finally, with no hesitation, he took off his clothes, so Fr. Seraphim rushed to put the adhesive dressing on and then quickly fled from the place, while Fr. Tadros began, very slowly, to put

---

32 *The Ascetical Homilies of Saint Isaac the Syrian.* (Boston, MA: Holy Transfiguration Monastery, 2011), 366.

his clothes on once again, before entering his cell, as though no one had seen him and as though there were nobody in the place except him.

His Blood Relatives

Throughout his time in the monastery, it was rumored that he was married and that he still had a daughter whom he was providing and caring for. This claim, however, was completely unfounded. On the other hand, he himself did not speak about his past. Nevertheless, he went out of the monastery to his town once a year, or perhaps every two or three years. In the seventeen years he spent here in the monastery, he went out to visit his family in Suhag four times. One of them lasted for a whole year or more, spending it in his old cell in his home.

He used to keep his share of the sugar, tea, and some canned food, so that he may take them with him to his family there [in his village]. The fathers used to assist him in organizing them, and then they would prepare a place for him and the things in any car that was leaving the monastery. The car would drop him at Tahrir Square, where he would stand perplexed, along with what he was carrying, until God sent him someone to help him reach his relatives in Waili neighborhood in Cairo or the train station which he would take, heading for Suhag.

And there in his home, he stayed in the same

room, wherein he had lived before monasticism. And it was there that he fulfilled his spiritual canon in full, without omission, according to the testimony of his relatives. Also, two of his relatives related that each of them went into his room, carrying food for him, on two separate occasions, but they did not find him there. The name of one of them is Angela Gabra and the second is Habashiya Moussa.

Throughout his stay there, he never visited anyone at all, except that he once visited H.E. Metropolitan Mina, to confess and receive a blessing. And if anyone of his family, or of the people of the village in general, wanted to visit him, he would permit them to come, but they had to refrain from prolonging their visit, otherwise, he had to leave them with the members of his family, to return to his cell, as he used to do before monasticism.

A group of his relatives, with their wives and children, once came to the monastery to visit him. He prepared a seating area for them in front of his cell, sat with them, offered to them what seemed suitable, and then sent them away in peace. When this recurred after several months, one of the fathers came to him, to inform him of their arrival. He answered from inside and learned from him that his relatives had come to visit him, and he promised that he would come out to [see] them. The marvelous thing is that he forgot the matter for several hours, until that father came to him again, knocking on his door, but Fr. Tadros rebuked him from within, asking him to go back to his cell and to his prayers, and so he did. After another several hours had passed, he came out, unhurriedly and calmly. The people were still waiting for him, and the hour was about four in the afternoon. When he saw them standing and waiting for him, he headed toward them and passed his hand over theirs [to greet them], in silence, and then he said to them calmly, "You were asking for me, and look, you have seen me. Go back to your homes now." And so they did, obeying [him], while he headed for the church, for the Prayer of the Eleventh and Twelfth Hours.

I also remember that a young man, almost thirty years old, knew the way to his cell, and so he began knocking on his door for a long time, with no one answering. And finally, a voice came from inside, asking who the one knocking was.

"It is so-and-so."

"Who is so-and-so?"

"I am your relative."

"I do not know anyone with this name."

"No, you know. I am so-and-so, the son of so-and-so." He was his second-degree relative.

"I said to you I do not know you. Nor do I know those whom you are talking about."

"Open for me, then, to only greet you."

"No, begone."

And the young man left, feeling sorry. For he was truly his relative, and he had met him before and sat with him outside his cell. And Fr. Tadros knew this, but he did not come out, nevertheless. Perhaps some looked to this as unfriendliness on his part, or [thought] that this may reveal instability of temperament. It seems, however, that this brother [that is, the young man] was visiting recently, and so Fr. Tadros feared that he would come frequently, whereas he was training himself to be free from everyone; therefore, he would not allow anyone or anything to take him away from what he is [engaged] in. The young man might feel sad for a little, but he will later realize that this father is a monk: he has his spiritual routine. And what might not be permitted for the regular person is permitted for the monk: for example, he might fast on non-fasting times, or eat outside the time for eating, or if he sleeps, or if he does not sleep, or if he neglects his clothes, or if he refrains from speaking; monastic life has its own character, being an untraditional [way of] life.

It is worthy of mentioning that this young man met him in Cairo at a later time, and he reproached him, but Fr. Tadros preferred silence and gave him no answer.

His Warfare with the Demons

Fr. Tadros succeeded in the discipline of the recluse to a very great extent, and he was harsh with himself.

His manner of life, especially the unceasing prayers and praises it consisted of, incited the resentment of the demons. All those who lived near him and those who passed in front of his cell would hear him arguing, protesting, and fighting with "others," who were the demons undoubtedly. We used to hear that daily, and he would sometimes yell, and other times he would curse them with rebuking words. And this struggle intensified around midnight. For sometimes it seemed that he was as though kicking the demons out of the cell, and this was during the nightly praising period. We also noticed that he would sometimes stop suddenly, and then with cautionary calmness, he would begin by saying, "Get out of here! Why did you come to this cell? Leave me alone; I am weak! Can't you find someone else to fight?" Then it did not take long before his voice would be raised, and we sometimes heard movement within, then he would cry out, rebuking them in the name of the Lord, and he would curse them, entreating the Lord to punish them, "May He burn you with fire! May He take vengeance against you! You are filthy!" And at the end of what resembled a battle, expressions of victory and gloating would resonate. Then he would soon return to what he was doing, continuing his prayer and praising.

This recurred on a daily basis, in the night more than during the day. H.G. Bishop Seraphim said that he once indirectly asked him, "Were you feeling a little tired last night, Fr. Tadros? And was there something disturbing you?" He, however, would evade speaking. And then he asked the same question in a different way, "What do I do about demonic warfare?" in hopes that he would perhaps induce him to talk about this matter. But it seems that Fr. Tadros himself realized this, that is, the desire of the inquirer to induce him to talk. Therefore, he resorted to silence, ignoring both the inquiries and the inquirer!

Did the demons envy him because of his godliness? Were they troubled by his unceasing prayers and praises, and consequently they diligently tried to hinder him from these? He, however, discerned this, and so he did not listen to them, nor was he overcome by these wars. And he did not even fear, having realized that the devil was like a vicious beast. If a person runs away from it, it pursues them, but if the person pursues it, the vicious beast runs away. And look, Fr. Tadros had remained faithful to the last breath, and see what disgraceful defeat has befallen the demons!

Most of us have looked at the phenomenon of his constant quarreling in the cell with others—I mean, the demons—as a great mystery: for at times he would reproach them with simplicity and contempt, and at other times, with a loud voice as someone who was expelling an unwanted visitor. As we listened, we felt that there were malicious guests within [the cell], looking at him with cunning and craftiness, like a blood-thirsty criminal. And they, that is the demons, were as though lingering in the cell, not wanting to go out of it!

H.G. Bishop Seraphim asked him about the pain from which he suffered in his left arm from time to time. He answered calmly, that while he was sitting to read or was standing to pray, all of a sudden, he felt as though someone else—he meant the devil—came close to him and then touched his arm, and at that, he felt a sudden pain, which would last for several days that followed.

4

His Final Days & His Repose

His Final Illness

He suffered from the traditional old age illnesses, yet he did not pay much attention to any of them. The complications of diabetes, however, plagued him near the end, but he used to endure silently and patiently. The sweet thing is that he was, one morning, seen standing with his back leaning against the Fort, imploring God and saying, "I am sick; believe me, I am sick—very sick. Have mercy on me, Jesus; heal me." And so he conveyed his feelings to God, with simplicity and amazing familiarity.

One of the fathers said that, three days before his repose, having become very sick, the fathers tried to gather around him, but he asked them, with seriousness and calmness, not to visit him; and so they left him, except one, who used to bring him food, leaving it at the door of the cell, and on the following day he used to carry it back as it was!

Fr. Isaiah of Baramous, who was responsible for the refectory, said that he heard he was sick, so he took some food on a tray and went to him. When he learned from within what he wanted, he asked him to leave the tray of food on the windowsill and to come at the same time the next day to take it. This recurred more than once, leaving the food and carrying it back untouched the following day, until a day came when he said to him, "Bring the tray of food and do not come back except after three days." So he obeyed and came on the third day; he called to him, but he did not answer as he was in the habit of doing. Then he pushed the door quietly, to find it unusually open. When he went in, he found him lying on the bed, exhausted. Then the fathers carried him to the hospital in Cairo.

Fr. Agapios passed by coincidentally and called him, but he did not answer. And when he noticed that the door of the cell was not closed as usual, he pushed it quietly, to be surprised by [seeing] him lying on a bed made of sackcloth beside the door. When he asked him how he was, he found him to be in bad health. And the fathers gave him some medications and food, but he did not respond to the medications, nor did he approach the food.

On the third day, his health deteriorated, and the fathers suggested that he be transferred to the hospital. And Fr. Agapios accompanied him to the Anglo-American Hospital in Zamalek district, Cairo. Upon arrival, the doctor performed a quick examination and advised them to take him back to the monastery at once, in hopes of arriving before his repose. The functions of the body—like the heart, kidneys, and liver—were about to completely fail, with the increase of the level of urea in the blood. As he was walking beside Fr. Agapios toward the car, he breathed his last, and this was announced by Fr. Agapios upon arrival at the monastery.

The Day of the Repose of St. Mary the Recluse

Fr. Tadros reposed on the first of February 1990, which remarkably coincides with the feast of the repose of St. Mary the Recluse. It was she who, after the repose of her parents, who were of the nobility of the city of Alexandria, refused to be married. Then she distributed her fortune, to join a monastery of the Virgin outside Alexandria. After fifteen years, she put on the holy schema and made her clothing of sackcloth. A short while after this, she took permission from the abbess to shut herself in the cell, so that she may receive a little food through a small opening she had made in the cell.

She continued in this discipline for twenty-two years, during which she restricted herself regarding fasting. And on the eleventh of the month of Tobe (the Feast of Theophany), she requested a little water from the Liturgy of the Waters (Lakkan), and she washed her face, then partook of the holy Mysteries on the twenty-first of the same month. Then she called the abbess, and the nuns also, asking them to come back to her after three days, at which they found her to have reposed. And this was on the twenty-fourth of Tobe.

Concerning spiritual struggle, Fr. Tadros said, in response to a question about this, that a monk should sleep for only two hours if he were a worker (physical laborer),[33] but if he were not so, then one hour is sufficient for him! It is known that the number of hours of sleep, with respect to the ordinary monk, ranges between five and seven hours per day.

And when Fr. Roweis one day asked him, when we were in the refectory, for a word of benefit for a young monk like himself. He asked him about his age, and he was thirty years old at that time. And then he advised him to be faithful in his discipline [or canon] from now, so that this may become a beloved work for him, that is, the [spiritual] struggle. And on a subsequent occasion he said to him, "When you were young, you would gird yourself and go wherever you wished; now that you have become old, another girds you and takes[34] you where you do not wish to go!" Perhaps he means that you are able

---

33 Literally: exerting effort.
34 Literally: walks.

now, while you are still young, to do what you desire of the various kinds of practices[35] before the time comes when you will not be able to do so.

It is known that there is a difference between desire and ability. There are people who have the desire but are not able to struggle; and there are others, on the other hand, who are able but do not desire to struggle! When a man is young in age, he is able to struggle, and toil, and keep vigils, and serve, and memorize the psalms and the Psalmody, and yet he may not have the desire to do so. But when he is advanced in age, the desire to do all of these might be borne in him, yet the ability would have abandoned him, because of the weakness of the body and because he has not become accustomed to labor.

On the vigil nights of Koiahk, every year Fr. Tadros used to come to church in his humble tunic,[36] wearing on top of it his old, bluish coat. He would sit quietly until the time came for the Koiahk hymn that he loved, and he loved chanting it every year in those vigils: "I begin in the name of the exalted God, and break the word of my critics, and explain about you from my mind, and I am not to be blamed," which is said after the Coptic Psali of the First Canticle. And he said it in a gentle and touching way, and he was moved by it at the same

---

35 Literally: struggles.

36 Or: *gallabiyah* or monastic garment.

time, and he would chant it with intense familiarity, as though he were its composer Abd Allah El-Abiary. In this hymn, the composer relates how the Virgin healed him of a disease that was about to cause him to lose his sight. We were in the habit of asking him every year, and with persistence, to say it, for we used to look forward to this blessed month to hear it from him. And I remember that in one of the vigils, while he was sitting beside us, he asked those around him, saying, "I am tired and I would like to say my hymn, so I may go back to my cell." They then asked him to chant another earlier hymn at its appointed time instead of the other. He also said this [other hymn] with joy, before returning to his cell. And this was the last vigil he attended with us before he reposed about two months later.

And now, when we are in church, in the Koiahk vigil, and the turn comes for that famous hymn, we remember him, looking to each other, asking for him the repose, and asking him to pray for us, for no one has given us delight in this hymn like he used to do.

Conclusion

This is the life of Fr. Tadros of the Monastery of Abba Paul, with all that it contained of virtues and weaknesses. And it is, by the way, extracted from a history written about him, which was penned by the author also. Consequently, not all the information related to him is recounted here, but rather what is suitable is published, while the rest was not included, for it is private and more suitable for the fathers of the monastery.

He still had, like all people, some remnants of the old man. H.G. Bishop Isizorus asks—and he is a reserved father by nature—and we also ask with His Grace: Were his moments of anger and some of his severe expressions directed against the demons, whom he thought were warring against him through the incidents because of which he was agitated? And does his being simple pardon him of the guilt of that, for he did not hate [anyone], nor was he guileful, and he would quickly return to his calmness and kindness, not harboring any grudge or hatred against anyone? For what is worst in him—or said in another way, the weaknesses in him—became manifest, and he was of course judged by others for them, while many of his virtues and feats remained hidden from us, and we knew none but the rare little. For combining between inner virtues and ideal conduct is a wonderful thing, indicating a good level of perfection. But if it were not possible to combine the two, then let the choice be first faithfulness in the discipline [or rule] and the care for one's salvation, and then the pursuit to please others.

In any case, he is considered one of the pillars[37] of

---

37 Literally: symbols.

monasticism in this generation, with respect to the discipline of the recluse monk; and we can imitate him, with respect to his seriousness, and to his death to the world and to everything and everyone around him. He brought back to our minds the image of the recluses of former times.

5

Examples of Recluses

Of the ascetics are those who left a kingdom and were content with a narrow cave wherein they lived joyously, eating a small amount of beans and dry bread. And of them are some who distributed their possessions and lived in the depths of the desert, amidst the dangers of beasts and the fluctuations of the weather. And of them also are those who abandoned the bishopric, to weep for their sins, resting their head in a burrow in an uninhabited cemetery.

And so many of the ascetics and recluses adopted various approaches[38] in their lives. For of them are those who lived in the shadow of a tree or on top of it, or who carved a dwelling in it, whom those in the Near East called the "tree-dwellers." And some lived atop a pillar, so that no one could reach them, and

---

38 Or: schools.

these were called the "stylites." And many occupied ancient Pagan temples, high in the mountains, where the ancient religions were located, to turn them into holy places, through the praises and thanksgiving they lifted up, and the tears they shed in them. And yet of them are those who restrained themselves with severe bonds, that perhaps they may find mercy before God.

We also hear about the famous recluse in the Abiyar region in Tanta, after whom the monastery there was named. The inherited tradition about him relates that the governor, while passing through that region, met this recluse, and he performed a miracle for him. When the Patriarch reposed, the governor suggested this recluse to the bishops if they desired to choose him as a Patriarch. The bishops came before the governor, along with the recluse, but the monk declined this, with the excuse that he was unworthy; and so they chose someone else, of those who were present.

Concerning women recluses, the scholar Theodoret wrote in his book *A History of the Monks of Syria* about two of them, Marana and Cyra. They abandoned their lavish living and their noble descent, to take for themselves a small fort at the entrance of the city of Aleppo in Syria, blocking the door with stones and mud. When the young women who were serving them desired to live in their way of life, they built for them a monastery near their fort. They spoke to them through an opening [or window], whenever they needed anything, through which they also received their food. While one of them spoke with the women visitors in the period of the Holy Fifties only, no one heard the other one speaking at all. Theodoret, who had seen them more than once with their permission, described them, saying that they wore long garments trailing on the ground. They spent more than forty years in this discipline, contemplating with much joy the heavenly Bridegroom, whom they always saw standing at a distance, His arms open to them.[39]

Theodoret also spoke of another recluse, who made for herself a hut out of millet stalks in her house. She clothed herself in a garment of hair and was content with boiled lentils for food. And she spent her time weeping as she prayed, out of the greatness of her love for Christ, her true Bridegroom.[40]

We also read in the history of St. Serapion, that he met a nun who was a recluse in Rome—through a conversation while he was outside her cell. She had spent twenty-five years in this discipline, without seeing anyone, and rarely did she talk with others. An old woman used to serve her, through an opening in the cell, through which she placed what she needed, in compliance with what she wrote on a potsherd. Abba Serapion counseled her of the necessity of

---

39 See Theodoret of Cyrrhus *A History of the Monks of Syria*, Price R.M., trans. (Trappist, KY: Cistercian Publications, 2008), 183–185.
40 See ibid., 186–189.

humility in thought and of perfect distrust in her righteousness.[41]

This is the same way that was followed by St. Anastasia the deaconess. She had disguised herself as a monk and went to Abba Daniel of Scetis. It seems that she had left her first cave, which was in the monasteries west of Alexandria, in pursuit of deeper stillness. Abba Daniel appointed for her a cave that was about eighteen miles away, in a deserted, desolate place. Every week, the disciple of Abba Daniel would go to her, reading what she had written on a potsherd, to come on the following week carrying what she needed. No one knew that she was a woman throughout the twenty-eight years she lived there. The fathers, however, learned this [that she was a woman] at the time of her shrouding.[42]

Likewise, Abba Bessarion placed St. Thais in a small cell, leaving a small opening in the wall, through which she received her food, which was a little dry bread and water.[43]

---

41 See *The Paradise of the Holy Fathers* 1, Budge A.W., trans. (London, UK: Chatto & Windus, 1907), 191–192.
42 See *The Anonymous Sayings of the Desert Fathers*, Wortley J., trans. (Cambridge, UK: Cambridge University Press, 2013), N.596.2.
43 See *The Paradise of the Holy Fathers* 1, Budge A.W., trans. (London, UK: Chatto & Windus, 1907), 140–142.

THE STORY OF THE MONK IN THE CELL NEXT-DOOR

St. Sedaros the Recluse in the Wilderness of Naqlun, Faiyum

Pope Benjamin, the 38th Patriarch, related concerning this saint, saying: During my journey in the desert, I visited a monastery for monks in Faiyum, and the number of its monks was low. They welcomed me warmly and joyfully. I asked them about the rest of their brethren, whether there was anyone who was sick and could not come. I was told about a monk who had been a recluse for twenty-five years, who had not opened the door of his cell to anyone. And he had said that the door of his cell no one would open except the saint Pope Benjamin. And so I marveled about what I heard, and I arose with the monks, heading for the cell of the recluse, and I called him. He answered, saying, "This is the voice of our father, the saint Pope Benjamin." Then I said to him, "My son, open the door." He answered me, saying, "Put your hand on the door, and it will be opened for you." As soon as I did this, the door was opened indeed.

The monk received me with joy and great honor, and said to me, "I thank God, that He has not deprived me of your blessing. Pray for me, my father, the saintly Pope."

I said to him, "May God bless you, my father, the blessed elderly monk."

He answered, saying, "May Christ our God have mercy on all of us, through your prayers, our saintly father."

After we had prayed, I sat down, and so did the monk. And his face shone with a halo of bright light. When I asked him about his life, he told me, saying, "I was from the town of Ashmunin. When my father, mother, and brother reposed, I lived with my sister. And she was godly, urging me to pray early every day. I worked as a laborer. And when my sister reposed, I worked on a boat that was going to Alexandria, on board of which there were godly Christians. I heard them talking about the virtues of the monks, their [spiritual] struggles, and their angelic conduct. When the boat arrived at Alexandria, and the day was Sunday, I went into the church [of St. Mark] and partook of the Holy Mysteries, being filled with longing for the life of holiness, and regret for my past days [spent] in negligence.[44]

"I met a monk outside the church and informed him about my whole story and my desire to become a monk. He told me that he was heading for his monastery, so if I wanted, I could go with him. And so I walked with him for a whole day, and on the following day we arrived at this place. Then the monk prayed for me and gave me spiritual words, and then put this garment on me, and he closed this door while I was inside. And he said to me, 'This garment will not wear out, and this door no one

---

44 Literally: idleness.

will open except Pope Benjamin on the day of your repose.'"

That monk Sedaros prophesied to me regarding the troubles that my children would face through the hand of the Chalcedonians. He also told me about the coming of the Arabs and my return to the residence of my Seat. And he prophesied, saying that I would consecrate a great church, in which many miracles would take place.

When I asked him about the saintly monk who had put the schema on him, and who had made him live in that cell, he said to me, "He did not make known his name to me. And I have asked God many times to make his name known to me. And so I saw that monk in a dream, and he said to me, 'Do not seek to see me in the flesh; you will repose and come to me after a particular period of time,' and he specified it to me."

After that, the recluse turned his face toward the east and asked me to pray for him and for all those who were in the monastery, that God may preserve them from all the plots of the demons. After that, he stretched his hand out and put it on my hand, then he drew it until it reached his face; so he kissed it, and I did likewise. Then he reposed in peace.

At that, I asked the monks to dig in the ground and bury him in his cell. When they had dug, they found a tomb, in which no one had been buried. It contained a coffin made of stones, whose length was that of the monk Sedaros. When they opened it, they found an engraving in Greek, "I, the poor monk Simon, when I lived in this cell and saw in a dream a man resembling an angel, who said to me, 'A believing man will come to you today, receive him, and pray for him, and ask him for a coffin of stones, that it may be a tomb for a monk of the saints, who will live in this cell after you. And preserve this coffin.'"

The blessing of the saint Sedaros the recluse may be with us all. Amen.

The Tower Recluses

Many ascetics inhabited military towers after they were vacated by the soldiers. In this, they were like those who lived in Pagan temples, as we have said. With time, towers were built specifically for ascetics to dwell in. Such a tower consisted of one story or more, and its height might exceed twenty-two yards. The first level was designated as a dwelling for the monk who is serving the recluse, while there is a wooden ladder connecting between the levels. And a fence is built around the tower, to keep the people away from the recluse, although he might sometimes speak with them through a window in the tower.

Such asceticism, disconnectedness, and silence might seem to be a way that is excessive and immoderate, and might be a reason for others' mockery and disparagement. In this, yet others might see obstinacy and unjustified fanaticism. But it is worthy of these and those to rather rejoice and be glad, for as the devil had led many astray through various kinds and ways, behold, here are people like this father, who are considered flowers and roses that are adorning the church, giving exhilarating colors to the entire fabric of the world.

Final Word

It is suitable of us that we call them blessed, and praise their manner of life, and rejoice in their struggle: we are one body, and each of us has a share in the goodness of the other. For one person walking in holiness certainly influences others, no matter how far they may be from him. For he rebukes the idleness of the indolent and the negligence of the heedless, and God accepts his prayer for others for the sake of his righteousness. Did the fathers not say that for the sake of the love of the one who did not sin, God forgave the one who sinned?

Even if he had a weakness or weaknesses, who of us is without sin, let him throw a stone at him first? God forgave the sinful woman, whom they dragged to Him by force. So how much more it is so with respect to a struggler who devoted his whole life, his bodily strength, his feelings, and the motions of his soul, so that he may offer a pure repentance accompanied by unceasing praise and fervent prayer like a blazing fire ascending to the heaven.

Who mocks the righteous—except the negligent? Who ridicules the struggler—except the one who is defeated through his weakness and misery? But the strugglers in general do not pay attention to those who wish to cast doubt in their work; nor do they have the time to spend on defending themselves. It is sufficient for them that they stand in the divine presence, and it is sufficient for them that God is pleased by their struggle and rejoices in their labor, and He receives them to Himself as a sweet-smelling incense.

Why are we surprised at these violent struggles of those righteous men for the sake of God, while we are not surprised at the tests and exercises of the special forces men, which are of uttermost danger, for the sake of achieving important targets successfully? Likewise are the champions of various sports, like weightlifting, running in races, and boxing, for the sake of achieving a new record. All this is for the sake of worldly glory and receiving a perishable and fading crown. However, those anchorites, recluses, and solitaries struggled for the glory that is imperishable, undefiled, and unfading, bearing in their bodies the marks of the Lord Jesus.[45] In any case, they lived in joy of heart and peace of soul, along with all these struggles, whereas such comfort is lacking in those who prefer the glory of

---

[45] See Galatians 6:17.

the world and its pleasures, choosing an easy life, far from their salvation and their eternity.

While some struggle to fulfill what is lacking in the afflictions of Christ in their bodies,[46] others have surrendered their bodies to all luxury and pleasure.

---

46   Colossians 1:24.

www.ingramcontent.com/pod-product-compliance
Lightning Source LLC
Chambersburg PA
CBHW071329040426
42444CB00009B/2110